# HOW TO WRITE AN
# OUTSTANDING
# CV

**Also by Andrew Knowles**

Become Really Effective on Twitter in Just 5 Days

Become Really Effective on LinkedIn
in Just 5 Days

# HOW TO WRITE AN
# OUTSTANDING
# CV

Your guide to writing the CV
that will help you stand out
from the crowd

## ANDREW KNOWLES

# Contents

# 1

# Your CV is YOU

**Your CV is you in your first round interview**

Don't make the mistake of thinking that your CV is just a piece of paper or words on a computer screen. When it's in front of the recruiter, your CV is *you*.

So what do you want your CV to do for you? You want it to convince the recruiter to choose you for the shortlist of people to be interviewed in person. This means your CV must make a compelling case for you being a strong candidate for the position they are looking to fill.

You'll read a lot about 'the recruiter' in this book. The recruiter could be the manager who's seeking a new member of staff for their team. Or they could be someone brought in to help with the hiring process, from the organisation's HR department, or they could be a recruitment consultant.

Who 'the recruiter' is really doesn't matter - what's important is that they're the one making a decision about whether your CV heads for the shredder or the shortlist. They're the person 'interviewing' your CV!

When you go for an interview, you dress smartly, because you know that first impressions count. And while good presentation isn't the whole story, it makes a big difference to the way that others think of you.

**Your CV needs to make a good first impression. It needs to come across as tidy, organised and professional.**

It only takes a recruiter about 30 seconds to know from your CV whether you're the right person to be added to the shortlist. Make sure your CV helps them reach a positive decision, fast.

**Your CV needs to answer the recruiter's questions quickly and clearly.**

During an interview, the recruiter expects to hold a coherent conversation with you. They ask you questions, looking for answers that they can understand and that give the information they are looking for.

In the same way, your CV needs to answer the recruiter's questions in terms which make sense to them. You can predict the sort of questions they'll have at this early stage:

- "What relevant experience do you have and how much?"
- "Do you have the appropriate qualifications?"
- "What sets you apart from the many 'average' applicants for the role?"

These are the questions that your CV must answer, clearly and succinctly.

**Your CV must be rich in quality of information, not quantity of information.**

It's surprising how many CVs are not designed with the recruiter in mind. Many are packed with information, as if the writer thinks that filling pages with lots of facts increases their chances of getting noticed.

In reality, it often works the other way around. If the recruiter cannot find the information they are looking for quickly and easily, they will rapidly lose interest. Your inability to present the appropriate facts, swiftly and cleanly, is already making a statement about your capability.

**A few key pieces of information, well presented, can result in your CV being shortlisted rather than dropped into the recycle bin.**

Never forget that your CV is your sole representative in front of the recruiter. It speaks for you and it needs to persuade the recruiter to give you a call or put you forward for the next phase of the hiring process.

# 2

# What does a recruiter want to see on your CV?

**Recruiters want candidates who add value**

Employers hire people who bring value to their organisation by doing things better. It might be by making more sales, helping processes become more efficient, improving customer relations or adding new skills to the team.

Recruiters do not want to see how many GCSEs or A-levels you have, how many sports teams you've played for or what you do in your spare time. These facts might help them to form a better picture of who you are, but they can't tell them whether you're the right person to fill their vacancy.

Try to look at your CV through the eyes of the recruiter. What would you be looking for if you were hiring someone?

The recruiter wants someone who will make a difference. They want to see evidence of this in your CV. Yes, evidence can include passing exams and getting qualifications appropriate to the role, but there's more to it than this.

## Your CV must focus on achievements

It must tell the recruiter, loudly and clearly: "This is what I have already done." The implication is that you can do the same, and more, in your new job.

This book shows you how to identify and record your achievements in a way that helps you stand out from the crowd.

## Recruiters want to see a stable job history

Employers don't want to go through the expensive process of hiring someone who doesn't turn up for work on the first day, or who leaves after just one month. This happens, and more often than you might think.

Having a history of holding down a job for several years will count in your favour. A stable job history demonstrates commitment, a quality that employers love and that recruiters always look for.

This need not mean you've done the same role for years, or even that you've stayed with the same employer for a long time. But a stable job history does require having a reasonable length of service, ideally two years or more, with each employer. If you haven't got this, try to include reasons that explain why you have changed jobs more swiftly. If you were made redundant, say so.

Recruiters hate seeing gaps in your working history. If you have a gap, you need to explain it. If you took time out to look after a sick parent or travel abroad, make sure you include this information in your CV. If you were unemployed, say so. Don't leave the recruiter guessing about what you were doing.

Repeated rapid job changes and breaks in your employment history need to be explained. Otherwise they don't give a good impression. Don't let your CV be discarded because your employment history appears incomplete or erratic.

## Recruiters want to see keywords

In the early stages of the recruitment process, when they're handling what could be hundreds of CVs, recruiters scan, rather than read in detail, the document you've submitted.

They may even employ software to do the job for them, usually called an applicant tracking system.

Whether it's a human or digital eye that first reviews your CV, they'll both be looking for the same thing - keywords.

These are the words, or phrases, which imply that you may be the right person for the job. These words could be previous or current job titles, professional qualifications, industries, locations or the names of specific systems or processes.

For example, a recruiter seeking a project manager may be looking out for terms like PRINCE2 or ITIL (these are formal methodologies for running projects), along with phrases such as 'team leadership' or 'meeting deadlines'.

You don't know what keywords the recruiter wants to see, but you can probably guess. Read the words used on the job advert or job description, if one is supplied. Take a look at the terms used on adverts for similar roles. These provide solid clues about the words recruiters are looking for.

Ensure the keywords are integrated into the text of the CV, and don't overuse them. The new generation of applicant tracking systems no longer just look for keywords; they also consider context, just as a human reader would.

## Recruiters don't want to see a photograph

Very few CVs submitted to recruiters contain a photo and adding one is unlikely to make a positive difference. In fact, it should make no difference, because recruiters are judging you on capability, not appearance.

If the recruiter decides to research you on LinkedIn or social media, there's a good chance they'll encounter your photo. But that's in a context where they expect it, rather than on your CV, where they don't.

# 3

# The structure of your CV

## Your CV must be easy to read

To make a great impression, your CV must be easy to read. Do all you can to make it really straightforward for the recruiter to find the information they are looking for.

The simplest way to do this is to break your CV into clearly marked sections.

The various sections on your CV should be:

- **Contact details** - these are really important.
- **Personal profile** - the headlines that tell what you have to offer.
- **Achievements** - a brief summary of how you've made a real difference or contribution in your current or previous places of work.
- **Career history** - where you have worked and what you achieved there.
- **Education and professional development** – work-related qualifications are particularly important.
- **Other information and interests** – such as relevant voluntary work or memberships of any trade or professional organisations.

Don't use lots of complicated boxes (these drive recruiters crazy) - clear, bold headlines are enough.

The titles of these sections may vary according to your personal preferences, but putting them in this order works well. By starting with a summary of you and your achievements, you are making it really easy for the recruiter to see if it is worth spending time reading the rest of your CV.

**An outstanding CV is long enough to convey the required information but short enough to be read in very few minutes.**

Knowing what to leave out of your CV is just as important as knowing what to put in it.

Almost every career can be summarised onto two sides of A4 paper, without needing to use a very small font. Almost all recruiters prefer CVs of this length, which are laid out clearly so the information they want is really easy to find.

# 4

# Contact details

**Make sure your contact details are clear and correct**

If a recruiter decides to get in touch with you, they want to do it there and then, while your CV is right in front of them.

And you want that too, because the moment your CV is relegated to the 'to do' pile, it's going to be forgotten.

It's vital that your contact details are very easy to see, absolutely correct and give the recruiter several options for getting hold of you.

Your contact details should include:

- **Mobile phone number.** This is the quickest way for a recruiter to reach you, so make sure it's presented very clearly and that it's correct. Get one digit wrong and you could miss that all-important call or text.

  A few people worry about privacy issues, particularly when their CV is posted onto a jobs' website and can be accessed by many different people. If this is a concern for you, and you're serious about getting a job, buy a pay-as-you-go phone just to take recruiter calls and texts.

- **Landline number.** This is a backup to the mobile, but you still need to be sure the recruiter has a good chance of reaching you on it, or can at least leave a message. Be careful about putting a work landline on your CV, as you don't know who'll answer it when a recruiter calls. Most recruiters are discrete, but don't rely on that.

- **Email address.** A recruiter will probably want to send you job descriptions and similar information from time to time. Make sure you're in a position to check your email regularly.

  To be taken seriously, your email address should have a professional tone. It's better to not use an email address which includes a pet name or makes a jokey comment about yourself, such as sexybeast666@hmail.com. (That's a fictional address, by the way, but it's not dissimilar to addresses some people use!)

  A quirky email address might be amusing to your friends, but it doesn't set the right tone when it appears on a CV. So if you have an email address that you think is perhaps a little unprofessional, don't use it on your CV.

  Again, if privacy is a concern of yours, create a temporary email address that you only use during the recruitment process.

- **Social media addresses**. Consider including your Twitter name or your LinkedIn website address on your CV. These show that you embrace social media, which in itself says something about you, demonstrating that you're forward-thinking and relatively open.

- **Postal address**. Even if you're willing to work anywhere, you should include your address, or at least some indicator of where you live.

  Some recruiters might take a look at your home address and rule you out of an opportunity based on geography. But if you give no clue as to where you are based, they are just as likely to exclude you.

  If you're flexible about location, state that clearly on your personal profile. It's not unusual for people to be willing to relocate for the right job.

**It's surprising how often people miss out essential contact information from their CV.**

Remember – in recruitment, time is of the essence. If you don't include a mobile number, a recruiter cannot call you or send you a text. By the time the recruiter has contacted you by email or on your landline, the vacancy may be filled.

# 5

# Personal profile

Do not start your CV with a list of exam results or details of your current job. They can come later. Instead, open your CV with a brief personal profile.

Here's an example of a personal profile:

Highly resourceful **Infrastructure Project Manager** delivering excellence in mission critical deployments across multiple regions and time zones for leading financial institutions, including Dolphin Bank. A **Prince 2 Practitioner** with over 15 years' experience of infrastructure support and transition project management roles.

Strong track record of delivering multiple complex projects in parallel, on time and on budget.

Technically strong experienced leader of diverse teams based in remote locations worldwide. Excellent communicator and negotiator, working with key stakeholders to achieve optimum mutual benefit.

Seeking a **contract role** which builds on the extensive skills and experience gained to date.

A typical personal profile comprises five or six sentences which summarise who you are and what you have to offer. It's a condensed version of the entire CV.

## Start strong

The opening line of your profile should sum up who you are and what you have to offer a future employer. Get this right and the recruiter knows almost immediately whether you're likely to be a candidate for consideration.

Include a job title in that all-important opening line and an indication of the areas you have worked in.

Examples of strong opening lines are:

> Award-winning **Retail Manager** with over 20 years' experience of building and leading teams in stores across the West End.

> Experienced **Technical Project Manager** delivering excellence in the oil and gas industry across Europe for over 15 years.

Both of these statements immediately tell the recruiter which roles the candidate has worked in, the level they have operated at and the geographical region they have experienced.

You can't condense everything into that first sentence, but you can put enough in there to entice the recruiter to spend a little more time on the detail.

## Don't underestimate the power of job titles

Choosing the right job title to describe your current and previous roles is important. Recruitment is driven by job titles, because they are short descriptions of the roles that people perform in the workplace.

Use job titles that are recognised by others in your industry. You are not obliged to retain the exact job title given by your employer. Organisations often use job titles that are unique to their business and which don't translate well into the outside world, so don't hinder your chances with a title that's meaningless to someone outside your current firm.

For example, a Technical Project Manager might wear a workplace badge saying Infrastructure Manager or Senior Operations Associate. These titles should be ditched when it comes to writing a CV. Use language that external recruiters understand - like Technical Project Manager.

## Completing your personal profile

- **Write it last.** Although your personal profile appears at the top of your CV, it is best written last, when you've had time to reflect on what you have to offer.
- **Back it up.** Every statement in your personal profile should be supported by detail further down your CV. The key skills that you include in your personal profile need to be backed up by achievements which demonstrate them.

- **Black-listed words.** Avoid using general terms, such as 'hard-working', 'enthusiastic' or 'I enjoy'. These don't really say very much.
- **100 word limit.** Try to keep your profile to less than 100 words. Having written it out once, go through it and eliminate any unnecessary words to ensure it's as short as you can make it.
- **Get a second opinion.** As a sense check, ask someone who knows you to read your personal profile and to confirm whether they think it sums you up. They might pick out an important positive attribute that you've missed out. Sometimes we find it too easy to undersell ourselves, so get help to remind you of your strong points.

Your personal profile might look something like this:

---

Highly motivated and tenacious **Health Project Manager** with a strong track record of delivering positive improvements in both private and NHS healthcare environments.

Excellent communicator who builds trust with clients and staff, with a high level of experience in motivating individuals and teams to succeed.

A highly effective negotiator used to identifying and working with key decision makers and stakeholders.

Seeking a role in the healthcare industry, where a commitment to delivering good quality support can be combined with a high level of organisational ability and an enthusiasm to see positive outcomes for clients.

---

PERSONAL PROFILE

This profile highlights the key attributes of the candidate:

- **Job title**. A project manager in healthcare, both public and private sector.
- **Key skills**. Communication, negotiation, motivating teams and organisational abilities. These should be supported by details, including career achievements, further down the CV.
- **Future role**. Looking for a job in healthcare.
- **Motivation.** Indication that they are driven by a passion for people.
- **Word limit**. This profile is 94 words long.

# 6

# The importance of career achievements

Having caught the attention of the recruiter with a great opening line and a short, sharp personal profile, your CV must now highlight your main career achievements.

Your achievements, both in previous jobs and your life outside the workplace, are the best indicators to the recruiter of the value you can add to an employer's organisation in future roles.

## What is a career achievement?

A career achievement is where you have made a positive difference in the workplace.

Achievements come in all shapes and sizes and they can be surprisingly difficult to spot.

You may already be wondering whether you have any achievements in your career so far. Perhaps you've never won any awards or received any formal recognition from your boss.

You're one of those people who just get on with their job and have not really achieved anything notable - or so you think!

## Who has career achievements?

**Everyone has achievements which can enhance their CV. This includes you.**

You may not recognise them at first, but the next chapter is designed to help you put together a list. By the time you have finished, you may even have too many to squeeze into a two-page CV.

However junior or mundane you consider your role or roles to have been, you have made a difference. Even if you simply did the same thing every day, that in itself is an achievement, because you were getting on with the job.

This truth is so important that it must be repeated:

**Everyone has achievements which can enhance their CV. This includes you.**

## Why are career achievements so important?

The recruiter wants to know about your achievements because they give an insight into the type of person that you are and the potential you have for a new position.

Every recruiter is looking for a certain mix of characteristics in a new employee. Every post that's being filled has a job title, such as Financial Controller, Operations Manager or Marketing Assistant. But behind the title lie the specific needs of the organisation that's hiring. Some of these needs may be spelled out in a job description, but others won't be written down anywhere.

It could be that the recruiter wants someone with the capability to overcome a particular problem, such as improving weak internal systems, rebuilding morale in a team, or handling a change in the level of business being undertaken.

Ideally, they want to hire someone who's dealt with similar issues in the past. By putting your achievements on your CV, they have a much better idea of what you can do and whether you're the right person for the job.

# 7

# How to discover your career achievements

A career achievement is where you have made a positive difference in the workplace. It's not just about winning awards or getting a special letter of commendation from your boss - although these are signs that you have achieved.

A career achievement is about how you have added value to your workplace. The recruiter wants to know what you've done and is looking for some insights into how you did it.

## Different types of career achievement

Achievements come in many different forms. Here are some of the ways in which they might appear:

- **Awards.** These are not achievements in their own right; they are badges of achievement. If you've been given awards, it's important to put them on your CV. But they must be accompanied by an explanation of the achievement that led to the award.

  **Promotions.** These are usually formally recognised, often with a new job title and increased financial rewards. But sometimes they just happen, when you realise you've taken on new responsibilities without any formal acknowledgement.

- **Meeting or beating targets.** If you're in sales, your CV won't be taken seriously if it lacks information on the sales targets you were given and the results you actually achieved. Always include authentic figures where you can as these give an indication of the size of your achievement. This isn't limited to sales; many other jobs also include the setting and measurement of targets.
- **Secondments.** Being asked to take on a role elsewhere in the organisation for a period of time is often a mark of achievement. It means you've been recognised as having particular skills or potential.
- **Improving processes.** This is an achievement that's often overlooked. It could be as simple as improving the office filing system. If it brought benefits, such as reducing the time taken to find information, it's an achievement.
- **Resolving problems.** It's easy to forget the times when a minor crisis occurred and you helped to recover the situation. It might have been a power failure, the sudden departure of a key colleague or the late delivery of an essential consignment. Whatever the problem, if you played a significant role in overcoming the difficulty, this is an achievement.
- **Leading teams.** Taking on the long or short-term leadership of a team is an achievement in its own right. You might have been formally appointed or simply rallied colleagues around you to deal with a particular issue.

## How to spot your career achievements

If at all possible, get someone to help you to find the achievements in your career. Have them read this chapter and then get them to ask you questions about your job history. Talking through what you have done helps unlock memories and remind you of details that you'd forgotten.

Here is a list of questions that your helper should ask you about every job you have ever done:

- What difference did you make in that job?
- Did you improve the way anything was done?
- How much benefit did your improvements bring? (Such as extra sales, reduced costs or time saved.)
- What gave you the most satisfaction in that job?
- What were you most proud of in that job?
- Were you ever asked to do a special role for a short time?
- What was the biggest lesson you learned in that job?
- Did anyone (your boss, colleagues, customers) ever commend you for anything?
- If you had reviews with your boss, what did you talk about?
- Did you ever turn a good idea into action in the workplace?
- Were you ever given any form of targets for performance, and how well did you perform against them?

If you can't get a helper, you can still ask yourself the questions. Get a pen and paper and scribble down everything you can think of when you look at the questions above.

Some of these questions may seem to cover the same ground, but they are all intended to get you thinking about previous jobs, and the longer you spend thinking about them, the more chance there is of remembering something that could be useful.

## A note from the author

I've interviewed hundreds of people, from apprentices to directors of household name firms, to collect the information needed to write their CV.

When I asked: "What was your biggest achievement in that job?" most said that they didn't have one. They had just "got on with what needed to be done". Even the highfliers struggled to think of "where they had made a difference".

But when I used some of the questions above, and started digging into their answers, every one of them discovered they had achieved much more than they had thought. "I'd forgotten about that" was a common response when we dug out another gem.

Your career is rich in achievements. There is no such thing as "just another day in the office". Every day, we solve problems for colleagues, customers or ourselves. We find better ways of getting things done and help others do the same. We put a stop to bad or outdated practices and we play with new ideas.

We learn, develop, improve. And the organisation we

work for gets a generous slice of the benefits.

Your achievements may not seem very impressive, but that's for the recruiter to judge, not you. Your responsibility is to make the most of what you've got.

Most of the other CVs they look at don't mention career achievements. Those CVs are dull lists of job titles, tasks performed and exam results. Your achievements, however small you think they are, help your CV to stand out and get you noticed.

## But I've never had a job…

Even if you've not been in the workplace for very long, or perhaps never even had a job, you still have achievements that deserve a place on your CV.

Think about the roles you have undertaken outside the workplace where you have made a difference. These could include positions of responsibility at school, college or university or things you have done in the wider community. They might include:

- Helping to run a youth group.
- Being a school prefect.
- Being on the management committee of a club at school or university.
- Organising sponsorship for a charity run.
- Helping out at a charity event.

Use the questions in this chapter to help you highlight your achievements in these roles which you can then use on your CV.

# 8

# How to write down your career achievements

By now, if you have followed the steps in the previous chapter, you should have a long list of career achievements scribbled down somewhere. The next step is to write out your achievements in a way that delivers maximum impact to the recruiter.

Your achievements can be added to more than one section of your CV. The best and most relevant are placed in the achievements section; others can be used elsewhere, such as in your career history.

**How you present your achievements can make all the difference to whether your CV gets the results it deserves.**

Here's an example of how one real-life CV looked before and after the achievements had been identified and written down. (The details have been changed to preserve the privacy of the individual.)

## Excerpt from the original CV

---

**Green Housing Association**
**Interim Financial Accountant**
**April 2011 to July 2012**

**Responsibilities:**
- Assisting with the preparation of the Statutory Accounts.
- Compiling and reporting on the Organisation's Energy Usage, costs, and value for money.

**Blue Housing Association**
**Interim Finance Manager**
**April 2007 to March 2011**

**Responsibilities:**
- Responsible for preparing the Annual Budgets for the Blue Group (including Cash flows) and presentation of same for approval by the Board
- Responsible for preparing the Statutory Accounts and subsequent approvals by the Board and AGM
- Responsible for preparing the Quarterly Finance Reports (including Management Accounts) for the Finance Committee
- Responsible for supervision of twelve members of staff
- Responsible for management of both the Internal and External Audit relationships
- Area Office (Croydon) - Manager
- Secretary to the Procurement and Efficiency committee
- Member of the Senior Management team

---

**And so on.** Did you read all of that word for word, or did you turn the page after reading a few lines, because it was boring? And what did it really tell you about the person on whose CV it appeared? Not a lot, except that they were an accountant, and you already knew that from the job titles. (And it also told you that they liked using random capital letters e.g. capitalising the phrase 'organisation's energy usage'!)

## Excerpt from the revised CV

**Achievements**

- Overcame major problems with the quality of accounting records at Green Housing to successfully produce financial accounts, in an interim role that resulted from major staffing issues.

- Delivered significant improvements in team performance at Blue Housing, despite facing a number of organisational issues:
  - Brought leadership and direction to a team that lacked motivation.
  - Successfully mentored staff, enabling them to fulfil their potential.
  - Worked through difficult issues, including fraud and a merger.

- Played a key role in the set-up of a new business in Florida, assisting a US organisation to establish a dry dock and yacht refurbishment operation. Set up the accounting system and provided management advice.

Hidden within those boring lines from the original CV are some valuable career achievements that recruiters need to see. These achievements were dug out through careful questioning (as outlined in chapter 7 above) and now appear in a separate achievements section as shown above.

Can you spot the difference? The first CV was for a boring accountant who kept the books and went to meetings. Recruiters see piles of CVs like that every day, from people in all kinds of work.

The second CV is for a proactive problem-solver, with accounting, management and leadership skills. This person is used to walking into demanding situations and getting results.

## Same person, same career history, different presentation.

The first version was a dull statement of responsibilities; the second tells stories about achievement. The details of their career history now appear further down their CV and include yet more achievements.

## Creating your summary of achievements

The recruiter has already been impressed by your personal profile, which in just a few sentences has given them a strong impression that you could be the right person for the job.

Now you might be wondering how to turn your list of achievements into short, powerful stories that give the recruiter an insight into what you have to offer.

To be effective, these achievements must have some relevance to the role you're going for, and must be relatively recent. In a near-perfect world, you'd tailor your CV to suit every application. (In a perfect world, you wouldn't have to apply for a job!)

Your achievements must have a strong opening statement and be written as succinctly as possible.

## Making the most of your career achievements

Here's an example of how to write an achievement on your CV in a way that gives a strong positive impression to a recruiter.

Let's start with a scenario. Several years ago, when employed in a sales role, you spotted an opportunity for your firm to benefit from a major building project. The result was that you sold a million pounds worth of floor tiles to the builders. (This scenario is based on a real-life example.)

The sales person initially recorded this achievement on their CV as follows:

> Instrumental in winning the Purple Tunnel Contract in excess of £1m.

At first reading this might sound impressive. But it's missing some key points and as a result, it's really underselling the achievement.

Let's rewrite the achievement to make a bigger impact.

**Start with the most important fact,** which in this case was the amount. Why is this the most important fact? Because it shows how much this achievement was worth to his employer.

---

Won £1m contract.

---

But you need to give it some context. A contract for what?

---

Won £1m contract for supply of paving products to Purple Tunnel project.

---

Okay, that's a nice one-liner. But can you add some depth to it? What were the particular issues that you had to overcome to win that contract? Were others after it and if they were, why was your bid successful?

---

**Won £1m contract** for supply of paving products to Purple Tunnel project, beating stiff competition through a combination of price, quality and commitment to excellence.

---

Now you have an achievement that's big and bold and tells a very short story. There's no harm in emphasising the keywords at the start, to catch the recruiter's eye.

## Don't be shy about your achievements

The British have a cultural problem when it comes to writing CVs. We don't like to blow our own trumpet.

If you want your CV to get noticed, you need to learn how to blow that trumpet as loudly and clearly as you can. If you don't, no one else will do it for you.

Take the example above, the £1 million contract for paving slabs on a major infrastructure project. Despite being a successful salesman, the writer of the original CV was unwilling to take full credit for delivering that deal. He was, after all, just part of a team.

While being interviewed for his new CV, he acknowledged that he played the key role in identifying the opportunity, putting together the bid and securing the deal. Yes, he'd had help and yes, it might still have happened if someone else had been doing his job.

But there was no denying his right to claim it as an achievement on his CV, and there was no reason to water it down, as he had done in the original version. Anyone who knows about selling in his industry would expect several people to be involved in winning a deal of that size, but they'd also expect that team to have a clear leader, someone with the vision to spot the opportunity, and the drive to get the result.

Apply this same principle to your achievements. Of course you should not claim credit where it's not due to you, but at the same time, don't undervalue the part that you played.

## How to write down your career achievements

You've now seen several examples of how to record your achievements on your CV. The key points are:

- **Keep each one as short as possible.** Write it, review it and rewrite it to reduce the number of words you use.
- **Start with the most important fact.** In the example above, the £1 million was originally at the end of the achievement, but the new version turned this around, because the size of the figure was important.
- **Don't undervalue yourself.** You're selling yourself here, not your team.
- **Be honest.** You'll probably be questioned about this achievement during an interview, so make sure you tell the truth.

Sometimes you need to add extra information to strengthen your achievement and you can do this by including additional bullet points. Here's another example:

---

**Delivered significant commercial benefits** by developing and implementing IT systems that cut manual processes from 2.5 days to 0.5 days:
- Worked with users to identify areas of potential business process improvement, specified systems required and managed contractor to deliver.
- Adapted efficient development practices to increase effectiveness of a service team.

---

The first line of this achievement could have been written as:

> Developed and implemented IT systems that cut manual processes from 2.5 days to 0.5 days.

But this wording is less effective, for two reasons. A strong achievement statement tells you why it's important, right from the beginning. 'Developed and implemented' is what was done, not what was achieved. The achievement was 'significant commercial benefits'.

The second reason it's less effective is that while it talks about cutting manual processes (i.e. saving money), the figures aren't that exciting. Cutting the time taken to do something from 2.5 days to 0.5 days is quite an achievement, but how much money did that save the business every year?

Unfortunately, this person didn't know, but they were confident that it was quite a lot, hence the decision to use the words 'significant commercial benefits'.

## Writing your summary of achievements

- **Be relevant.** Your achievements paragraph should only include those achievements which are relevant to the role you are aiming for.

  For example, if you have worked as a teacher for ten years but now want a job in management, you need to find achievements that illustrate your capability in that area.

This might include a role on the senior management committee or extra responsibilities, such as managing the special needs provision in the school. Awards you may have received for being the best teacher as voted by the pupils are probably not relevant.

- **Demonstrate capability.** Give the recruiter a sense of what you can do.

  For example, a salesperson needs to demonstrate that they are able to make sales and must include achievements that illustrate this, whilst an accountant needs to indicate how they can add value rather than just 'do the job'.

---

Achieved target sales levels.

---

Improved credit control.

---

- **Show the scale.** Put the achievement in context with numbers and time scales.

---

Achieved target sales levels of 100 deals every month in 2011.

---

Improved credit control leading to a reduction in average debtor days from 45 to 35 days.

---

- **Indicate how it was achieved.** This may illustrate how you work or summarise initiatives that you have taken.

> Achieved target sales levels of 100 deals every month in 2011. Created my own leads and followed them up, signing an average of 10 new customers a month.

> **Improved credit control** leading to a reduction in average debtor days from 45 to 35 days by implementing a formal process of timed follow-up for invoices.

## More examples of achievements

> **Saved £50k per year** in printing costs through improving internal communication with marketing teams and negotiation with suppliers.

> **Awarded salesperson of the year** in 2012 for best performance against target. Achieved £120k sales compared to a target of £100k.

> **Reduced staff turnover** by 50% by allowing team members greater involvement in operational management, including introduction of weekly team meetings and performance targets.

**Improved stock control system** at major industrial client as part of a 6 month secondment.

**Successfully led project** to evaluate the different options for a new computer system.
- Managed team of 5 people.
- Successfully collected and collated the relevant information by the deadline.

# 9

# Employment history

If the recruiter likes the look of your profile and your achievements, the employment history section is where they'll head next.

The story of your working life tells them a lot about what you can offer to another employer. But it can also give them reasons why they should bin your CV on the spot. So take care.

This is likely to be the single longest section of your CV, so it's important to get it right.

## Keep it simple

This part of your CV can quickly become a jumbled mess, as you try to show information about who you worked for and what you did.

Use a clear, simple layout, avoiding complicated tables of information or trying to get clever with columns. The recruiter wants to scan your job history quickly; they don't want to learn how to read a complex grid of facts.

## Stick to the important information

One of the big questions for this section of your CV is what to put in and what to leave out.

Your natural inclination is probably to include too much. You want the recruiter to know about everything you've done, in case it might be useful. You wouldn't want to leave out the one piece of information that would convince them to shortlist your CV, would you?

Your worry is misplaced. If you've got the right skills and experience for the job, this will come across in a well-written CV. The absence of one minor fact is unlikely to make a difference.

## How to write down your work history

Always start with your current role and work backwards. The recruiter doesn't want to wade their way down twenty years' of employment history in order to find out whether your present or most recent role is relevant to the job you are applying for.

Start by making a list of all the jobs you've ever done and put them into date order, with the most recent at the top and the oldest at the bottom.

Make sure there are no gaps in the timeline, particularly in the recent past. Recruiters don't like to see gaps in your career history, because it makes them wonder what you were doing during that time.

If you do have gaps, perhaps because you took time out as a full-time parent, went travelling for a year or couldn't get a job, explain this on the CV.

When you've had several jobs with the same employer, you need to decide whether to include each role separately. If the changes show career progression or promotions, that's a great story to tell. On the other hand, if they're just changes in title, or the jobs were so long ago that they have little relevance to the role you're after now, don't bother.

Remember that recruiters are most interested in the work you've done over the last five years or so.

## Including achievements in your work history

As you list the different jobs you have done, remember to record your achievements, not just your responsibilities.

You've already recorded your main career achievements in the achievements section of your CV. Your work history section allows you to add yet more achievements.

Don't be tempted to fill this section with material copied from your old job descriptions. A job description is the document used by recruiters and employers to list all the tasks they expect someone to do.

Using parts of your old job descriptions, if you have them to hand, is quick and easy, but it also misses the point of an effective CV.

A job description sets out what you were expected to do in a particular role; it doesn't tell the recruiter what you actually achieved.

Job descriptions are also pretty dull to read and recruiters can spot them a mile off because of the way they are written.

What is more impressive than a job description is a list of achievements because this brings your work history to life.

Examples of achievements include:

- Being seconded to a particular team or office for a short while.
- Improving the efficiency or profitability of your team or department.
- Developing new systems or processes to cut costs or get the job done more effectively.
- Hitting or beating targets.
- Receiving awards for achievement.
- Developing or leading a team.

**Add specifics to your achievements**, to help the recruiter get a feel for their scale. Record how many were in your team, by how much you beat targets or by how much you improved efficiency.

## An example

Perhaps the best way to illustrate an achievements-led work history is to look at how one CV was adapted from being accurate but dull to being accurate and dynamic.

Take a look at the CVs on the next two pages. On the left-hand page is the original CV. It is all factually correct, and gives some insights into the type of business worked in and the levels of responsibility.

But it's also quite vague. What does 'manager for very busy London store' actually mean? Was it a small shop somewhere in the suburbs, or a frantic retail emporium in the heart of the West End?

On the opposite page, the CV has been rewritten to highlight career achievements.

**2009-Present**
**Co-owner and director**
**Red Carpet Ltd – UK franchise of Bateaux Rouge**

- Bought franchise for an American luxury brand, supplying designer handbags.
- Involved in every area of the business including purchasing, marketing, public relations, and technological development.
- Director in charge of staff management.

**1994-2009**
**Fashion Extras plc**

**2000-2009**
**Store Manager**

- Manager for very busy London store.
- Responsibilities included marketing and advertising campaigns.
- Responsible for all personnel management including arrangement of shifts and holidays, managerial floor cover and staff training.

**1994-2000**
**Store Manager**

- Manager for London store selling high quality fashion accessories.
- Responsibilities included marketing and advertising campaigns.
- Responsible for all personnel management including arrangement of shifts and holidays, managerial floor cover and staff training.
- Also responsible for two other London stores simultaneously.

**2009-Present**
**Co-owner and director**
**Red Carpet Ltd – UK franchise of Bateaux Rouge**

- Initiated launch of successful American luxury brand into the UK market, supplying designer handbags.
- Grew UK business from scratch to achieve a key position in European group with €22m turnover.
- Implemented innovative technology solutions to manage production processes, cutting turnaround on bespoke items to 2 weeks.
- Plays a key role in every aspect of business including wholesale sourcing and purchasing, marketing and public relations.
- Manages a team of 20 staff across 2 locations.

**1994-2009**
**Fashion Extras plc**

**2000-2009**
**Store Manager**

- Responsible for very busy flagship Oxford Street store (8,000 sq. ft.).
- Grew turnover from £2m to £6m, initiating a number of marketing campaigns which boosted sales.
- Introduced innovative team leadership and training methods to motivate staff.
- Led a staff team of up to 30.

**1994-2000**
**Store Manager**

- Headhunted to manage West End store (5,000 sq. ft.) selling high quality fashion accessories.
- Grew turnover from £1m to £2m.
- Managed up to 15 staff.
- Given additional responsibilities for a further two West End stores simultaneously.

Can you see the difference? The recruiter can immediately see the level of responsibility the candidate achieved, through facts such as how many staff they managed, the level of turnover (sales) they were responsible for, and the size of shop they ran (in square feet - a figure that means something to those in the retail industry).

It also highlights achievements, such as speeding up the production processes and motivating staff. This also sets up obvious questions for an interviewer to ask, such as "Can you tell me more about these innovative leadership and training methods you introduced?"

Because the candidate has laid the ground for these questions, they can also prepare answers in advance, making the prospect of an interview less daunting.

# 10

# Education and professional development

The recruiter has been wowed by your profile, impressed by your achievements and is very pleased with your career history. Now they're looking at your qualifications, in part to see whether they put ticks in the right boxes, and in part to see what further insights they can gain into your potential.

The 'ticks in boxes' is because many employers insist that those shortlisted for interview have specific qualifications or experience.

## Keep it brief

Don't waste time and space listing all the schools you've been to on your CV. At most, include the name of the last place you were in formal education, which is probably a college or university.

School exam results are equally unimportant, unless you achieved them in the last five years or so.

Recruiters are not interested in how many O-levels, GCSEs or A-levels you got fifteen or twenty years back, so leave them off your CV.

There's no harm in letting the recruiter know that you're a graduate, so if you have a degree, include some information about that. Show the name of your degree, and where you studied.

However, do not include this if you did not complete your course or failed your degree. Surprisingly, some people do choose to include this. But this doesn't add anything to your CV and probably detracts from it.

There's no value in listing all the different modules you covered in your degree, unless it's relatively recent and highly relevant to the job you're applying for.

You are not obliged to tell the recruiter what class of degree you achieved. If it's a first class or 2:1 you want them to know, but if it's less than that, you may want to leave it off.

If you wrote a thesis or dissertation on a subject that's highly pertinent to your chosen career path, you could choose to mention it.

## Professional development

Education above degree level may well be relevant to the type of job that you're looking for, so include this where appropriate. This does not mean listing every course you've ever attended, but highlighting those that are the most appropriate.

Include the qualifications, certifications and professional accreditations you've achieved, but again, only where relevant.

## No qualifications? Don't worry!

You may be one of the many who struggle with this part of their CV. Your academic achievements are few, if you have any at all, and the jobs you've held haven't offered much opportunity to obtain formal qualifications. If this is you, don't panic!

Lots of senior figures in many organisations don't have a string of letters after their name, or rows of certificates on their wall. What they do have is a track record of success in doing their job.

If you really have nothing to put in this section of your CV, then leave it out entirely. There's no value in drawing attention to what you haven't got. Instead, put more effort into strengthening the other sections of your CV, such as your achievements and career history, where there's lots of good news to share.

# 11

# Interests, referees and other information

**Don't use this section to pad out your CV**

The recruiter wants to know whether you're the right person for the job. If you've done something in your own time which could help convince them of this, include it.

Avoid writing meaningless statements about what you like to do, such as 'socialising with friends', 'watching films' or 'reading'. If these are the highlights of your life outside work, leave them off your CV. It's not that there's anything wrong with them, but they don't add anything to the picture of who you are.

On the other hand, perhaps you've set up or run a group or club, or you enjoy organising charity events. These could be right for your CV, if they enhance the image you want to portray.

**If the only reason you're writing about hobbies and interests on your CV is to fill space, don't do it!**

## What's in and what's out

Here are some other ideas about what to include and exclude in this section of your CV.

Consider including:

- Membership of any club that's in line with the job that you want.
- Any hobby that fits well with the job you're looking for and that you participate in regularly. Be prepared to answer questions about it, because your interviewer might share a common interest.
- Involvement in charitable activities, as this says something about your willingness to put yourself out for others.
- Activities that show you are interested in continued self-development, such as training courses that you have attended outside of work.

It's best to avoid including:

- Detail about your personal circumstances, such as being a single parent, or recovering from illness. While you may want a potential employer to know this, it's probably better to bring this up at the interview stage.
- Achievements which some recruiters might not regard favourably. For example, founding or running a group involved in online video gaming might be a good example of your skills, but some recruiters may dismiss it as a waste of time.

## Referees

Referees are the people who the recruiter can contact to get a second opinion about you.

Some recruiters like to see the names of referees on a CV; others don't. Some won't bother to contact referees, while others will follow them up.

One approach is not to name referees on your CV but to include a line such as 'Excellent references available on request'. This could be useful if you want to choose different referees depending on the specific job you're applying for.

It's important to get permission from referees before passing over their contact details. It's also wise to warn them if a recruiter is likely to be in touch.

Choose wisely when asking people to provide references for you. Previous employers are usually a good choice, because they can comment on your capability in the workplace. Unfortunately, many firms are reluctant to provide references in case it leads to legal action for misrepresenting you.

Failing that, find people who will be positive about your character and who have some credibility in society, such as accountants, teachers or lawyers.

Don't use people you've had no dealings with for years.

If you're planning to put your CV on a jobs website where it could be seen by many others, don't include the names and contact details of your referees. While they give permission for you to pass their details to a recruiter, they're unlikely to be happy with these details being published to what could be a large audience.

## Presenting useful information that doesn't fit anywhere particular

You may want to include some snippets of useful information which don't have a natural home in any specific section of your CV, particularly if you choose not to have an interests section.

The ability to speak a foreign language, having a full, clean driving licence, or the possession of some other skill could be a positive attribute on your CV, but it may not be obvious where it should go.

The answer is to put these facts where they fit most naturally.

For example, for a role where having a driving licence is clearly essential, you could highlight this in your personal profile.

# 12

# An outstanding CV is extremely easy to read

**Your CV needs to be easy for people and computers to read**

In their search for the right candidate, recruiters can be required to scan hundreds of CVs a day. That's 'scan', not 'read'. When a job advertisement attracts hundreds of applicants, taking even five minutes to read every CV submitted would keep them at their desk for days.

By sheer necessity, recruiters have learned to scan CVs very quickly, running their eyes across the page to pick up the keywords they are looking for. Because of the repetitious nature of this job, it's increasingly being handed over to computers to perform, using CV reading software (often referred to as an applicant tracking system). Many of the world's leading organisations now take this approach.

Alternatively, the initial review of all CVs is a job delegated to junior staff working to a strict list of criteria, such as specific qualifications and keywords.

The thought of being just one of hundreds applying for a particular job can be pretty disheartening. Especially when the initial sifting of CVs is going to be a fairly mechanical process. But if you're a strong match for the job requirements and your CV is well-constructed, you're still in with a good chance.

Many of those applying are unlikely to be well-suited to the role - online applications make it too easy for job seekers to chase hundreds of jobs, many of which are outside their core expertise. These are the CVs that get weeded out in the early stages of the recruitment process.

## Clear and simple; boring yet effective

Recruiters, whether reviewing CVs by eye or with software, prefer every CV to be laid out in a similar way. A CV that tries to be different, forcing them to scan it in a different way, could lead to key facts being missed.

A well-designed CV must be very easy to read. The layout might look boring, but this is where being dull is the most effective way of getting the message across.

Avoid using logos, images or what you consider to be an attractive mix of colours. Black and white text is all that recruiters want to see.

## The two-page CV

Recruiters like CVs that are on just two sides of A4 paper. Any less and it looks a bit thin. Any more and you're saying too much. This principle applies whether you've been in work for a couple of years or a couple of decades.

Recruiters dislike long CVs for many reasons: they take too much time to read; the information that recruiters are looking for is difficult to find; and the CV's length indicates that you find it hard to get to the point.

You might wonder how you're going to get everything onto a CV that's just two pages long, and includes lots of white space.

If you've been in the workplace for a couple of decades, you've probably amassed a substantial career history. Your various job descriptions alone amount to several pages. Add to that the training courses that you have attended, the certificates you've received, an impressive list of key skills and a smattering of hobbies, and you've almost got enough material for a short book. Your challenge is to strip the facts back to basics and fit them onto two sides of A4 paper.

Alternatively, you could feel your CV is so short that it needs padding out with everything you can think of, in order to make it look respectable. In this case, work hard to dig out more achievements that you can add. But if the facts don't stretch to two pages of text, don't force it to look longer than it really is.

Whatever your situation, don't make the mistake of including irrelevant information on your CV.

## Use a standard font

You'll probably write your CV on a computer. Recruiters will probably read it on a computer or tablet or even on their smartphone.

If they're reading from a computer screen, most people prefer to read text written in a font that's easy on the eye. Arial, Tahoma or Calibri are popular choices. Font size 11 or 12 is preferred, particularly if the CV is going to be printed out, which could happen, particularly in the later stages of the selection process.

Clever or arty fonts, even when used only for titles, might be eye-catching, but they're also very annoying. Avoid design flourishes, such as titles aligned to the right of the page or graphics that you think help your CV to look different.

Ask a recruiter what they think of these little forays into graphic design and most respond negatively.

## Use a clear, simple layout

The way to make your CV stand out is by including excellent content, presented clearly and concisely.

Don't try to be clever - use a plain, simple layout, so the recruiter can easily find what they want. A CV that's laid out badly confuses recruiters.

Break it down into the clearly labelled sections that we have already talked about, such as employment history, training and qualifications and achievements.

Make sure the information isn't crowded. In particular, avoid long sentences and long paragraphs. If your CV contains a block of text that's more than four lines long, find a way to break it up.

People find it hard to read a chunk of text. We've all become used to scanning web pages, picking and choosing the information that's useful to us and moving on. Recruiters read CVs in the same way. They glance at the page and try to absorb the key facts before reading the detail.

Don't put text into paragraphs that are more than four lines long. Keep sentences short.

Avoid adding tables of information to your CV. You

should be able to present everything with a heading and then a list. If you create a table with multiple columns, it takes the reader a moment or two to understand what's going on. It might be very clear to you, but that's because you designed it.

## Don't be afraid of white space

An empty page is pure white space. As you fill it up, the amount of white space diminishes. Many people don't like to leave much white space on their CV. To them it feels like the silence in a conversation, a space that's uncomfortable until it's filled.

Do not be afraid of having a lot of white space on your CV. You might consider it wasted space, where you could put more exciting facts about yourself. But the truth is that the key points about what you have to offer can easily be spread across two sides of A4 paper, with plenty of room to spare.

Remember to present the most important information first. This is why your personal profile - the short, succinct summary of what you have to offer - is at the top of the first page. It's what the recruiter reads first and that alone could determine whether they continue down the page.

If you think your CV looks 'too busy' then it probably is.

## But doesn't an unusual CV get you noticed?

We've all heard the stories of people who've drawn attention to themselves by submitting a highly creative CV. Like the IT technician who created a CV in the style of a 1960s horror film poster, or the journalist with a CV designed to mimic a Facebook page.

While both got their CVs featured on blog posts, it's telling that the former found his eye-catching style worked initially, but since the economy got tougher from around 2008, he admits that it's not getting him interviews.

The Facebook-style CV seems equally unsuccessful. One potential employer called it "brilliant" and shared it online, but didn't give her the job.

Ask a recruiter which they prefer - plain or creative - and they'll go for plain every time. Occasionally the highly original approach draws in some extra attention, but that's mainly for the style, not the content.

Think of it this way. Sometimes a complete unknown turns up to audition for a film or a show, gets noticed and becomes a star. It happens, but not very often. A visually attractive CV occasionally gets someone noticed and as a result, they land a fantastic job.

The chances of that person being you are pretty slim. It's safer to play the CV game by the rules the recruiters prefer.

**Keep it simple and boring.**

# 13

# An outstanding CV has good spelling and grammar

## Use a spell checker

Despite almost every CV being written on a computer, and probably being written using software that includes a spell checker, it's amazing how many CVs include spelling errors.

Every day, recruiters bin CVs that have failed the review process because of spelling mistakes. A candidate who claims to 'pay great attention to detail' yet overlooks easy to fix errors on their CV is making a costly mistake.

Misspelling slightly difficult words, such as 'proffessional' shouldn't happen, because a spell checker easily identifies the error. Typing mistakes, such as using a correctly spelt word in the wrong place of, are a little harder to spot. Did you notice the rogue word in the previous sentence? Look for the extra 'of'.

Many of us miss these tiny mistakes, but not everyone. If the recruiter has an eye for picking out typing errors, spelling mistakes, rogue words and dodgy apostrophes, this could mean the end of the road for your CV.

## Ask someone else to read your CV

The best way to find these mistakes is to get someone else to read your CV, very carefully. Don't be embarrassed to ask a friend or family member to help. Your next job could depend on it.

Ask the same person to look at the grammar you've used. This can be rather daunting, because most of us don't really know many rules of grammar.

The best approach here is to think about how each sentence reads. If in doubt, read it aloud. If it sounds okay, it probably is okay. But if you think it sounds wrong, take a moment to find a better way to express yourself.

The recruiter is unlikely to be any more of a grammar expert than you are. But how well you write tells them something about you, and you want to give the best possible impression.

If you really struggle to express yourself clearly in writing, it may be worth paying a professional CV writer to do the job for you. See Chapter 19 for more information about this.

# 14

# An outstanding CV is a great match for the job on offer

### Aiming your CV at the right job

The clearest, most achievement-packed CV still fails if it's not aimed at the right job. When a recruiter is looking for an IT Project Manager to lead a team of software developers, they don't want to see a CV from an Engineering Project Manager who builds bridges.

Part of the process of delivering an outstanding CV is to target appropriate jobs.

The digital age makes it too easy for candidates to apply for positions that they do not have the right experience for. You just click on a button, attach your CV document and hit 'Send', in the hope that the recruiter recognises your potential, even though your background isn't what they were looking for.

A badly aimed CV is a waste of everyone's time. It can also be hugely demoralising to apply for hundreds of jobs online and get no response, even when the reason is that you don't have anything like the right qualifications or experience for those vacancies.

## Matching your CV with the job requirements

It pays to take the time to look at the information about the job vacancy you are interested in and to see how closely it matches what is on your CV. You may want to tweak your CV slightly to ensure it highlights the exact skills and experience that the recruiter is looking for – assuming that you have them, of course.

When your CV is a good match for the role on offer, and the relevant facts are easy for the recruiter to find, you stand a much better chance of getting noticed.

The internet age has made it much more likely that you will be invited to apply for a job before you see it advertised. That's because, as part of the job hunting process, you will probably upload your CV onto one or more recruitment websites. Recruiters search through these sites looking for people with the right skills and experience for the vacancies they have to fill.

If a recruiter finds your CV on a recruitment website, they'll usually contact you to discuss the role before submitting your CV to the organisation that's looking to hire. Before this happens, it is worth reviewing your CV in the light of the information supplied by the recruiter and considering whether the document needs enhancing.

While your CV may have been good enough to catch the recruiter's eye, it may stand a better chance with the hiring organisation if you tailor it to meet the requirements of the specific role.

Increasingly, recruiters are searching for potential candidates on social media sites such as LinkedIn, so it's important that your LinkedIn profile matches your CV. Chapter 20 tells you more about LinkedIn.

**An outstanding CV persuades the recruiter to pick up the phone and call you right away.**

Do recruiters often find a perfect match between a CV's content and the requirements of the job? No.

But near-perfect matches are more common. Recruiters get excited by CVs that are an excellent match for the vacancy they are trying to fill. They quickly get on the phone because they don't want to miss the chance of securing an almost ideal candidate for the role.

However, you need to be wary. Some recruiters are a little over-enthusiastic, or inexperienced, or both. They can read things into your CV which aren't there, particularly if they're in line for a fee for finding the right person.

When it comes down to it, you, not the recruiter, are in control of your job hunting. Feel free to ask the recruiter why they think you are a good match for the position and if you disagree, don't be afraid to walk away.

# 15

# An outstanding CV sells YOU!

## Struggling with self-promotion

One reason why many people find it hard to write their CV is their reluctance to sell themselves. You may be reading this book because you want to put together the best possible CV, but you might also be one of those who find self-promotion a daunting prospect.

Take a moment to think about why that should be. Are you good at what you do? Are you a reliable, hard-working and honest person who would be an asset to your employer? Are you committed to doing a really good job?

If the answer to these questions is 'Yes', it's important to get a right view of yourself and what you have to offer. You have a value to your future employer and you have a duty to yourself to let them know about that value.

Of course it's important not to oversell yourself, but don't undersell either.

## Recruiters are looking for achievers

Recruiters seek people who have achieved, and will continue to achieve, in the workplace. They're not looking for people who can get the job done; they want people who can get the job done well. If that's you, you need to tell them, because no one else is going to promote you to them. And you can be sure that lots of other job hunters are putting themselves forward as the ideal candidate.

Your CV needs to come across as confident, but not cocky. As indeed do you, when it comes to being interviewed. You need to be certain within yourself that you can do the job. Don't be intimidated by the nature of the role you're going for or the size of the business you're applying to. If you've read the job description and think you can do it, go for it with confidence.

After all, what's the worst that can happen? The recruiter might decide your CV is not right for that role or that there are too many other candidates even better qualified. It's frustrating when you're told that your CV won't be considered further, or worse, you don't get a response at all to your application. But that's much more likely to happen with a weak, bland CV than one that's full of confidence and enthusiasm.

**Put aside your reservations and let your CV sell you.**

# 16

# An outstanding CV does not resort to lying

## Keep to the facts

Almost every recruiter tells you it's wrong to lie on your CV. There might be the odd one or two who are happy for you to embellish a few facts if it helps you to get the job and them to land the commission. But most want you to keep it truthful.

A recruiter who thinks you are worthy of consideration for a role will probably look you up online. If you have a LinkedIn account, they'll compare your profile with your CV, and note any significant differences.

Many recruiters don't take up references and those that do won't usually ask a referee to validate your CV in detail.

However, a good interviewer will spot discrepancies between your CV and the story you tell them. Of course, if you make it to interview, your CV has done its job and it's down to you to secure the role. But if your CV contains untruths, these may be exposed by the interview process.

And it doesn't stop there. If you have the good fortune to be hired, your boss or colleagues may have enough familiarity with your CV to spot differences between what you say about your employment history and what's written on that document.

Presenting yourself in the best possible light on a CV is perfectly acceptable, but it's important not to embellish the truth to create a false impression.

# 17

# CV checklist

This checklist is a summary of what to put in and what to leave out of the different sections of your CV. The sections of your CV are:

- **Contact details** (these should always be at the top of your CV)
- **Personal profile** (this is the 'headline' section of the CV, so it must be right at the top, after contact details)
- **Achievements** (these are your career highlights, so should follow the personal profile)
- **Career history** (this section can come before or after 'Education and professional development', as you prefer)
- **Education and professional development**
- **Other information and interests**

## Reminders for each section of your CV

### Contact details

- A mobile phone number, on which you can be reached quickly, so the recruiter can send you a text or phone you.

- An email address with a professional-sounding name, so the recruiter can send you information.
- Your postal address, so the recruiter knows whether you are in the right place geographically.

## Personal profile

- Remember to use a universally understood job title.
- Give clear information about what you have to offer.
- Indicate the type of role you are looking for.

## Achievements

- Three or four short, punchy statements about when you've made a real difference at a place you have worked.
- Where possible, include some measure of the value of the difference, such as actual sales achieved, time or money saved, or some other benefit.

## Employment history

- Include a summary of your employment history, starting with your most recent role. Don't leave the recruiter guessing at what you've been doing for the last few years.
- Do include your achievements, demonstrating that you're able to get results.
- Don't include job descriptions. They might fill up the space nicely, but that's all they do; talk about what you achieved rather than listing your duties.

- Don't include gaps. Make sure all your time is accounted for, including career breaks.

## Education and professional development

- Do include relevant qualifications, as these could be one of the factors used to quickly weed out the least suitable candidates.
- Don't include details of your education before secondary school. It's irrelevant.
- Don't include a list of every training course you've ever attended. Only include those that are relevant to the role you are applying for.
- Don't include skills you acquired decades ago which have no practical use in today's workplace.
- Don't include qualifications you began but never completed.

## Other information and interests

- Do include volunteer work and achievements in out of work activities if they are relevant to the role you want.
- Do include either named referees or a line such as 'Excellent references available on request'.
- Don't include general statements about your interests. They do nothing except take up space.
- You don't need to include your date of birth. It's not required and it's illegal for recruiters to discriminate on the basis of age.

# 18

# Five reasons why your CV might be binned

**Recruiters can sometimes make what seem to be illogical decisions**

Recruiters are inundated with CVs. One job advert can attract hundreds of applicants. Even when they haven't advertised a vacancy, many firms receive speculative CVs almost daily.

To cope with the high volume of CVs they receive, recruiters need to find ways of dramatically reducing the numbers to something more manageable. They often resort to making decisions based on criteria which, on the face of it, seem illogical and could see the best applicants being rejected.

**What's good for the recruiter may be bad for you**

Imagine a recruiter is faced with 200 CVs for a particular job and ten of them are from candidates good enough to be shortlisted. To find these ten as quickly as possible, the recruiter rejects all those who lack a specific qualification or who can't spell professional.

It may be that the recruiter eventually finds seven or eight CVs that are good enough to shortlist, meaning that two or three good quality candidates have been lost because they did not meet the criteria set by the recruiter. That's hard luck for those two or three, but the recruiter still has plenty to choose from.

On top of this, recruiters are human and sometimes make irrational and illogical choices, particularly if they have two candidates that it is hard to choose between. While discrimination on some issues is illegal, there is no law to say that you can't be rejected for a job because you don't know how to use apostrophes correctly.

Whilst you cannot prevent a recruiter from making irrational decisions which lead to your CV being rejected, you can minimise the risk of this occurring by following the tips below.

Here are some of reasons why your CV might be rejected by a recruiter, even though you could be the ideal person for the job:

## 1. Spelling mistakes

Everyone makes typing errors and there's no rule that says a brilliant salesman never mixes up 'there' with 'their'. But this doesn't stop recruiters from discarding CVs simply because they contain just a single spelling mistake.

**Use a spell checker and read your CV out aloud to rid it of errors.**

## 2. Unusual presentation

Pink, scented paper, a colourful curly font or a quirky layout definitely makes your CV stand out. Unfortunately, it also dramatically increases the chance of it heading toward the reject pile.

**Keep your presentation simple. It is the content that counts.**

## 3. Lots of long paragraphs

Recruiters want to read your CV quickly and they soon get lost in dense blocks of text. If you want them to keep reading, make it easy for them.

**Keep your paragraphs short and surrounded by lots of white space.**

## 4. Your email address is odd

What you might consider a playful or light-hearted email moniker may just irritate, or even offend, a recruiter. That's enough to consign your CV to the bin.

**Keep the email address that you use for applying for jobs professional in tone.**

## 5. You support the wrong football team

Sport can be very emotive and it has been known for a recruiter, when faced with two equally well-qualified candidates, to choose one over the other because of the team they support.

**Avoid putting the name of the team you support on your CV.**

# 19

# Using a professional CV writer

## Paying someone else to write your CV

If, even after reading this book, you're still struggling to put together a CV that you're not embarrassed to present to a recruiter, maybe you should consider giving the job to a professional.

It costs money, but think of it as an investment in your career. If a professional CV gets you a job earning thousands more than your previous position, or with better prospects, or which gets you back into employment, then it's money well spent.

A professional CV writer will, if they are any good, be able to distil what you have to offer into a short, sharp and effective document.

## How much should you pay for a professional CV?

Unfortunately, you don't always get what you pay for when it comes to professional CV writing. You can pay hundreds of pounds to get a document that could have cost you a lot less, if you'd known where to look.

Realistically, a good quality CV is going to cost in the region of £100 to £250. Think about it − if you want the CV writer to spend several hours writing your CV, including taking time to conduct an interview with you, you should expect to pay a reasonable amount of money.

A good CV writer is going to be an experienced professional, so you can't expect them to work for a few pounds per hour. Six hours at £25 per hour is £150. Experience says that researching and writing a CV usually takes from four to eight hours.

## You can pay too much, or too little

The big CV writing companies can charge hundreds of pounds. That's because they have offices to pay for and huge advertising budgets. The CV writing market is very competitive. The person who writes your CV probably receives only 10 to 20% of the fee that you pay.

Small CV writing companies have sprung up by the hundred and many are one-man-bands. They offer a complete CV for as little as £25. If you consider how many hours of time that's buying you, you can see that it's not a lot.

The best way to find a good CV writer is through referral. Ask friends or use social media, such as Twitter, to seek out recommendations. Ask potential writers to explain how they work and what their process is for ensuring that you get what you want for your money.

# 20

# Going beyond the CV with LinkedIn

## LinkedIn profiles

LinkedIn is a networking website which has become very popular with recruiters over the last few years. It is now one of the first places they turn to when looking for someone to hire.

If you don't know what LinkedIn is, take a look at it. Some call it Facebook for business, but if you're not a Facebook fan, don't let that put you off.

LinkedIn allows you to create a profile for yourself, in sections which are very similar to a CV. You can add details of the exams you've passed, your career history, a summary of your skills and more.

People you have worked with, or for, can add recommendations to your LinkedIn profile. These provide further insights into what you can offer recruiters. They can also endorse your skills, giving you added credibility.

If you think LinkedIn is just another place to put CV information, think again. It's much more powerful than that.

## Get found through LinkedIn

Ask any professional recruiter about their use of LinkedIn and they'll tell you it's become a key tool for finding candidates.

LinkedIn has a powerful search engine which allows recruiters to track down individuals who have the skills they are looking for. You can improve your chances of being found by building a network of contacts within LinkedIn and by getting involved in some of the many online discussions which take place there.

This book is not about how to use LinkedIn. But if you're serious about finding another job, you should take a look at it.

## Tips for using LinkedIn

Make sure the information in your LinkedIn profile matches your CV. If a recruiter finds your CV through another source, there is a good chance that at some point in the hiring process they will look you up on LinkedIn. If the information on your profile does not match your CV, it could raise concerns.

Add a good quality profile picture. While your CV does not include a photo, your LinkedIn profile can and should. Use a good quality head and shoulders photo which will strengthen your image as a hardworking employee. Avoid holiday pictures or camera phone snaps of you at a party.

Ask for recommendations. It's quite normal to ask colleagues or others you have worked with for a recommendation on LinkedIn. Don't be embarrassed - other job hunters won't be.

Get involved in discussions. Maximise the chance of being spotted by a recruiter by participating in some of the many discussion groups on LinkedIn. These help bring you to the attention of other LinkedIn users and increase your chances of appearing in searches.

You can discover more about how to set up and use LinkedIn in my ebook: 'Become Really Effective on LinkedIn in Just 5 Days'.

# Appendix: Example CVs

Example CV1: Arthur Clennam
- Operations Manager

Example CV2: Amy Dorrit
- Sales Executive

Example CV3: Bob Cratchett
- Chartered Accountant

# Arthur Clennam
Address
Mobile telephone number    Telephone number
Email address

## PROFILE

Highly effective **Operations Manager** with many years' experience of running highly efficient IT services teams and operations. Has worked across a variety of sectors including **data centres** and **retail. Fully qualified.**

Proven record of delivering excellence in customer relationship management, project management, team leadership and management of resources. Highly skilled across a range of disciplines including **major account management, regional service management and national help desk operation.**

Seeking new opportunities to build on skills and knowledge gained to date, and committed to adding substantial value to a wide range of organisations.

## SELECTED ACHIEVEMENTS

**Consistently achieved** service delivery targets across a variety of different organisations, beating KPIs and demonstrating a results-oriented approach:
• Achieved 95% SLA and productivity targets at Red Ltd.
• Consistently the highest performing Area/Regional manager, winning management achievement awards at White Ltd for service excellence.

**Successfully established** national infrastructure for serving £3m pa account at Blue Ltd, including onsite team of four, and managed the account for over two years:

- Secured extension of contract from three to five years without going to tender.
- Achieved renewal of multi-million pound contract, having been brought back in to restore customer confidence at end of first five years.

**Maintained low turnover** of both staff and clients during 20 years at Blue Ltd through high quality of communication, attention to detail and customer focus.

Successfully turned around failing team of seven working onsite on £1.5m pa contract, re-motivating staff, returning the account to profitability and restoring the client's confidence in Yellow Ltd.

**Significantly increased productivity** and quality of area team at Blue Ltd by actively managing the training of engineers and focusing on team building:

- Improved First Time Fix rate to 86% and Fix Within Contract rate to 94%.
- Lifted both rates from below target to above target.
- Ensured processes were in place to deliver continuous improvement.

**SELECTED TRAINING COURSES**

Six Sigma Black Belt (2008)
IT Service Management Certificate (ITIL) (2004)
Prince 2 Project Management Foundation Course (2002)

## EMPLOYMENT EXPERIENCE

**2010-Present**
**Data Centre Planning and Installation**
**Manager/Service Delivery Manager**
**White Ltd**

- Headhunted to establish and monitor standards and policies to ensure consistently high quality of server installations in data centre.
- Delivery manager of new utility-based (cloud computing) email service, £2m pa.
- Eight month assignment managing £1m customer contract, running a team of seven staff at the customer site and working with helpdesks in India and USA.

**2009-2010**
**Project Engineer/Project Manager**
**Yellow Ltd**

- As Project Engineer, managed resources and resolved major recruitment issues.
- As Project Manager for two £1.5m work streams, ensured progress remained on target.
- Successfully managed one work stream through a major milestone that ensured further public sector funding was accessible.

**2007-2009**
**Field Services Manager**
**Red Ltd**

- Integrated newly acquired businesses into organisation.
- Built new team in Scotland to replace subcontractor, improving quality of service to customers.

**1987-2007**
**Blue Ltd**

**2003-2007**
**Service Desk Manager**
- Established newly formed service desk supporting customers across the UK.
- Performed due diligence on sale of service desk business to third party.

**1999-2003**
**Regional Manager**
- Delivered IT services across England with a budget of £1.5m and team of over 180 staff.
- Supported Purple plc Account Manager to ensure £3m contract was retained.

**1995-1999**
**Area Manager**
- Managed contracts of up to £250k and up to 30% annual growth.
- Significantly improved First Time Fix and Fix Within Contract rates.

**1992-1995**
**Service Account Manager**
- Set up and ran infrastructure to manage new £3m pa contract with Purple plc covering 900 stores.

**1990-1992**
**Area Supervisor**
- Managed a team of 20 staff supporting customers across southern UK.

**1987-1990**
**Senior Customer Engineer**
- Delivered onsite support to customers, resolving a wide range of issues.

**Excellent references available on request**

# Amy Dorrit
Address with postcode
Home phone number   Mobile phone number
E-mail address

## PROFILE

Ambitious and extremely commercial **Sales Executive** with an excellent track record of achievement and a passion to succeed. Has experience in **cold calling, field sales, telephone sales** and **retail sales**.

Naturally resourceful and innovative, looking to maximise all available resources to achieve sales success. Establishes excellent relationships with customers and skilled at asking probing questions in a friendly manner, extracting detailed information about customers' needs. Extremely capable at matching products to needs and successfully promoting these to customers to win business.

Looking for an opportunity to make an outstanding contribution to a quality and profit-focused company, building a strong sales career on the skills and experience acquired to date.

## SELECTED ACHIEVEMENTS

**Consistent sales achiever**, meeting or beating targets on a regular basis:
- Always one of the top two sales executives at Zebra Ltd every month.

- Best performing month was over 200% of target (of £10k sales).
- Increased sales at Elephant Ltd by 30% in first month through consistent approach to building customer relationships in order to drive up additional spend.
- Consistently beat weekly sales targets at Camel Ltd.

**Successfully negotiated major sale** at Camel Ltd, valued at £25,000:

- Identified possible customer by researching high-growth businesses with potential significant IT networking needs.
- Identified correct contact within customer and initiated discussion of their networking needs.
- Alongside technical colleagues, was instrumental in developing the solution for the client and negotiating a profitable deal.

## KEY SKILLS

- Telephone and field sales expertise.
- Cold calling.
- Experienced at closing deals.
- Excellent objection handling capabilities.
- Quick learner, investing personal time to maximise product knowledge.
- Researches customer needs using multiple sources.
- Creates solutions to customer requirements and promotes them effectively.
- Organised and disciplined; excellent time management.
- Proven capability for self-motivation.

## EMPLOYMENT EXPERIENCE

### Zebra Ltd
### Sales Executive
### 2010-2012

- Responsible for telephone and face-to-face sales of business training courses to customers.
- Telephone cold calling and follow-up of customers from free seminars, to promote three-day training courses.
- Active sharing of accounts and opportunities through meetings and maintenance of high quality records.
- Management of database of customers and opportunities, using Goldmine.
- Achieved sales of 200% of target, and consistently in the top two sales executives every month.

### Elephant Ltd
### Customer Services Assistant
### 2009-2010

- Part-time role held while studying for MBA.
- Responsible for taking bets on a wide range of sporting and other events, and dealing with customer complaints and enquiries.
- Proactively sought to promote business by creating a welcoming atmosphere for customers.
- Increased sales by 30% in one month by creating a larger spend per customer.
- Targeted monthly promotions of gaming machines, encouraging customers to participate and driving additional revenue.

**Camel Ltd**
**IT Sales Executive**
**2006-2009**

- Joined Camel Ltd, a leading systems integrator and solution provider, specialising in LAN and WAN networking and supply of desktops and servers, based in Sheffield.
- Initially responsible for prospecting and cold calling potential customers.
- Once experienced, took on field sales role, visiting potential customers and negotiating sales.
- Managed existing accounts and proactively pursued additional business from established customer base.
- Created and managed own database of customers and leads.
- Consistently beat sales targets.

**EDUCATION & TRAINING**

MBA - International Management, Sheffield Hallam University, 2010.
BEng (Hons) – Electronics, Sheffield University, 2006.

**References available on request**

# Bob Cratchett FCA

Address with postcode
Mobile phone number    Home phone number
Email address

## PROFILE

Successful **Chartered Accountant** delivering excellence for almost 20 years as a Partner in accountancy practice. Now looking for **Accounts Manager, Finance Director** or similar senior role in the **charity** sector.

Technically strong with extensive experience of ensuring compliance with accounting and auditing standards, including latest SORPs. Maintains high quality of working practices across a multidisciplinary team. Excellent track record of auditing and preparing charity accounts and Charity Commission returns.

Forms and leads successful teams to undertake specific projects, including audits and more specific investigations. Consistently focuses on delivering maximum benefit to the customer, providing high quality advice and recommendations to improve efficiency and reduce risk.

## SELECTED ACHIEVEMENTS

**Ensured ongoing compliance** with ever-increasing body of regulation and best practice for auditing, accounts preparation and charity reporting.
- As Audit Compliance Partner for £2m firm, maintained up-to-date knowledge across the audit teams.

- Provided audit advice to other partners in the firm.

**Saved clients thousands of pounds** in taxes by advising on options and reliefs available to clients with varying circumstances.

- Advised charity client on correct accounting and reporting procedures when making payments to volunteers which could be construed as wages.
- Advised sole trader on specific reliefs for their particular profession.

**Identified £50k fraud** being committed by client's employee, through detailed analysis of accounting records.

- Liaised with client's offices in the UK and USA to investigate and locate source of the fraud.
- Advised on improved procedures to reduce future risk.

**Improved efficiency and cut costs** by implementing new procedures for managing audits and accounts preparation for clients.

- Replaced inconsistent working methods with standardised working papers and procedures.
- Introduced Management Letter for clients, advising on issues raised by audits, before this became a professional requirement.

**Maintained training office accreditation** with multiple accounting bodies, ensuring compliance with relevant standards and practices.

- Supplied professional bodies with all required information and liaised on regular training audits.

- Ensured all trainees and other relevant staff had access to appropriate training and CPD (continuing professional development) resources.

## QUALIFICATIONS

Fellow of Institute of Chartered Accountants in England and Wales, 1999.
Member of Institute of Chartered Accountants in England and Wales, 1989.

## PROFESSIONAL EXPERIENCE

**2012-Present**
**Career Break**
Travelling and teaching English in India and Thailand, with major charity.

**1992-2012**
**Palm, Birch, Chestnut and Co**
**Partner**
- Joined as partner designate and became partner within two years.
- With fellow partners, ran £2m pa Chartered Accountancy business with up to 20 staff.
- Managed a portfolio of clients with turnover of up to £20m, including a number of charities and medium-sized firms of solicitors based in Birmingham.
- Supported other partners in the firm with provision of advice on compliance issues on audits and accounts preparation work.

- Assisted clients in raising up to £120k funds and facilities from banks.
- Reviewed clients' accounts and tax computations, providing advice on areas where costs or tax liabilities could be reduced further.
- Drafted returns to the Charity Commission for clients.

**HR**

- Responsible for HR issues in the firm, including recruitment, employee welfare and disciplinary activities.
- Successfully resolved situation arising from new employee with forged references and qualifications.
- Created staff handbook and other supporting documentation.
- Managed staff disciplinary actions, including issuing of warning letters and conducting meetings until issues resolved.

**Training**

- Managed all aspects of staff training and development, including ensuring trainee accountants achieved required experience and skills.
- Gave presentations to staff as appropriate.

**Health & Safety**

- Responsible for all health and safety matters in the firm, including preparation of risk assessments and liaison with external contractors.

**1986-1992**
**Oak, Beech and Co**
**Audit Trainee, Audit Senior and Audit Supervisor**
- Promoted through from Trainee to Audit Senior and Supervisor.
- Qualified as a Chartered Accountant.
- Performed wide variety of audit and accounts preparation work for selection of organisations.

**ADDITIONAL INFORMATION**

- Full clean driving licence
- Qualified First Aider
- Qualified to teach English as a foreign language (TEFL)
- Currently learning Italian

**Excellent references available on request**

# About the author

Andrew Knowles is a freelance writer and speaker helping businesses to communicate more effectively with their customers, in print, online and through social media.

Andrew has written over 250 CVs for a wide variety of individuals ranging from graduates to directors of household name businesses.

His understanding of high quality communication is founded on over twenty years' experience in a variety of client-facing management roles in both commercial and not-for-profit organisations.

He advises firms on social media strategies and gives highly effective presentations on social media to businesses and professional groups.

Andrew has written social media guides for Twitter and LinkedIn that draw on his extensive experience to help others learn and master these social networks quickly and easily. 'Become Really Effective on Twitter in Just 5 Days' and 'Become Really Effective on LinkedIn in Just 5 Days' are both available from Amazon as ebooks for Kindle.

Andrew lives in Weymouth, Dorset, with his wife and business partner, Rachel, and a varying number of student daughters.

He can be reached through his website: www.writecombination.com or on Twitter, as @andrew_writer.

www.ingramcontent.com/pod-product-compliance
Lightning Source LLC
Chambersburg PA
CBHW051340_70526
45166CB00002B/886